# I Made It Out
# On Broken Pieces

*From a Broken Piece
to a Masterpiece*

*by*

## Dr. Taketa Williams

WWW.TAKETEAWILLIMASMINISTRIES.ORG

**I Made It Out On Broken Pieces**

ISBN : 978-07212575-70
Copyright © Dr. Taketa Williams
Website: www.taketawilliamsministries.org

Printed in the United States of America. All rights reserved.

Published by Impact Ministries Inc.
1-888-424-9673
Website: www.experienceicc.org

# *Dedication*

This book is dedicated to my family. We have been through so much and survived many things. The enemy rushed into our lives like a flood, but the Spirit of the Lord lifted up a standard against him. We've faced peril and have experienced much distress. We've encountered many storms and survived shipwreck, but I'm so thankful that we made it out on broken pieces.

To my husband, Apostle Roderick Williams:

I love you with my whole heart. You are an incredible man of God, a dynamic husband and a wonderful father to our children. God made me for you and my earnest desire is to continue to please you. Making you happy gives me great joy. My endeavor is to make you smile all the days of our lives. I love you forever and ever.

To my children Shakeyla and Roderick II and my granddaughter Sha'nila:

Thank you for sharing me with the world and allowing me to minister to God's people. You all have been so patient and so kind. You could have been selfish and kept me all to yourselves, but you recognized the gift of God in me and pushed me to share it with others. You are the best children that a mother could ever desire. God blessed the fruit of my womb to give birth to precious children like you. You are incredible and amazing. I love you so much.

# TABLE OF CONTENTS

# Introduction

*"And the rest, some on boards, and some on broken pieces of the ship. And so it came to pass, that they escaped all safe to land." - Acts 27:44*

The pressure of perfection is a force that people experience all the time. Everyone desires the perfect life, perfect marriage, perfect family, perfect job, perfect health and perfect peace. In pursuit of perfection, tragedy comes to reduce us to living a life of faultiness so that our dreams can be defective and our mission can malfunction. The enemy simply doesn't want your life to work as God planned. The devil doesn't want you to reach your divine destination; therefore, he sends ongoing opposition to deter you and get you off course.

The adversary tries to ride on the wings of adverse winds in an attempt to cause your life to go in reverse, opposite of God's divine plan. He uses belligerent storms to break you down and hostile hurricanes to take you under. While sailing on the voyage of life, he's praying evil prayers against you hoping that you shipwreck and that your life falls to pieces. He wants your ship to break and your boat to sink. He desires for you to drown by the cares of this world and be overtaken by the waves of the sea. Like Jonah, the devil is hoping that you are swallowed up by a great fish so that you will never see what your ultimate end will be.

What I love about God is that even if your ship breaks, He will allow you to make it out on broken pieces and although a great fish may swallow you up, the Lord will make the fish spit you forth to the place that you're supposed to reach. Your times are in the Lord's hands and your life is hidden in Christ Jesus. God will only allow but so much to happen to you and everything that works against you will ultimately work for you.

God's thoughts and plans toward you are good and not evil. He purposes for you to fully function without dysfunction and conquer the very possibility of malfunction. The foundation of this book, "I Made It Out On Broken Pieces," was established on the basis of Acts 27. Paul, an Apostle of the Lord Jesus Christ, is on a voyage with other prisoners. While in the midst of the sea a violent storm and strong winds strike the ship. The blows are so vicious that the hits causes the ship to wreck. God used devastation to help Paul and the other prisoners to reach their destination. They made it out on broken pieces. Whatever you are going through in your life, you will make it out. Things may fall apart, but God is going to make good use out of your broken pieces. After you survive, He will then turn your broken pieces into Masterpieces.

# CHAPTER 1

*Surviving the Storm*

# SURVIVING THE STORM

The world is made up of many different and diverse types of people. There are over 7 billion people that exist and no one person is the exact same. Despite all of our various colors, creeds, cultures, nationalities, backgrounds and walks of life, there is one thing that we all have in common; we are all faced with challenges, difficulties, expostulations and storms. Storms are not prejudice. They don't care if you are black or white, tall or short, educated or un-educated, rich or poor. Storms see no color. They look beyond one's status, disdain one's educational background and are not influenced by one's financial state. They work the same in all of our lives – when they arrive, they come to accomplish a purpose regardless of the person.

Not one human being on the earth is exempt from being opposed by remonstrative storms; they're simply a part of life. In fact the word of the Lord tells us in Job 14:1 that, *"Man born of a woman is of few days, and full of trouble."* However, as believers we find joy in the fact that trouble doesn't last always. Though trials may be many, the Lord knows the trajectory of our life. He knows the way we take and when we are tried He purposes for us to come out as gold. There is nothing that our God does not know. He is Omniscient, He is All-Knowing and He knows absolutely all things. He is intimately acquainted with our purpose and our pain, our struggles and our successes, our up rises and our downfalls; He knows.

Knowing that storms occur, we must endeavor to live a *Storm Proof Life*. Our faith must be so strong that we are not distressed by storms neither are we impressed by their workings. Being Storm Proof is like being Fire Proof. The fire may emerge however; those things which are Fire Proof are not impacted by the fire. The three Hebrew Boys mentioned in Daniel 3:19 were Fire Proof. They were thrown into a fiery furnace and the fire was turned up seven times hotter. It is obvious, according to the Word of the Lord, that they were never touched by the Fire nor did they come out smelling like smoke. They were Fire Proof because of their faith. They relentlessly believed in the Lord their God, the God of their salvation. Being Storm Proof is quite the same. The storm may rise, but because of your faith you cannot be overtaken by the demonstrative effects of the situation. Though winds may blow strong, there is a confidence that rises within the Storm Proof believer that declares, *"My faith is stronger."*

Often times those without *Storm Proof Faith* are devastated by the boisterous winds and catastrophic seasons of torrential rain. The reason being is that their level of faith does not match the category of their storm. It is vitally important that you know the category of your storm. Meteorically, a storm is typically accompanied by rain and strong winds. The speed of the wind determines the category of the storm. As speed increases, the category increases and as the category increases, the possibility of disaster and potential destruction increases as well. You must know how fast your winds are moving and release your faith to move faster. Your faith must outrun the speed of your storm. My question is, *"How fast is your faith?"*

Let's examine actual hurricane winds. Hurricanes have five different categories and each level has different results. A Category 1 Hurricane moves at approximately 74-95 mph. Winds moving at this speed can cause damage to well-constructed frame

**P❋WERP❋INT**

**You must know how fast your winds are moving and release your faith to move faster. Your faith must outrun the speed of your storm.**

homes and can cause damage to roofs, shingles, vinyl siding and gutters. There could also possibly be more extensive damage to power lines and poles which may result in power outages that could last a few or several days. Look at this from a spiritual perspective. A hurricane storm has the potential to damage the well-constructed frame of your life and the roof over your head which is symbolic of protection. Your frame is that which holds everything together. If the frame collapses, then your life begins to fall apart. As strong winds aggressively move in your direction, you must declare the Word of the Lord over your frame and command the structure of your existence to stand and not be moved. The bible declares in Hebrews 11:3 that the worlds were framed by the Word of God. If the Word of God can frame the entire universe, then surely the Word of the Lord can hold together your life's frame in the time of storm to keep your world from caving in.

In addition, a Category 1 Hurricane in many cases has caused damage to power lines and caused power outages lasting for a few to several days. If you are not Storm Proof, wayward winds and tumultuous thunders that move in your direction will attack your Spiritual Power Line and knock your power completely out. If you're not girded up, you will find yourself in a place where you're weak, exhausted, restless and powerless by everything that's going on around you. You will be robbed of the stamina you need to endure and the strength you need to overcome. You will ultimately become feeble and faint, and if you faint in the day of adversity then your strength is small (Proverbs 24:10). You're too big for anything about you to be small. The Lord wants you to have big strength, big faith and big victories. You must increase the category of your faith to supersede the category of your storm. If your hurricane is a Category 5, then your faith has to be at least a Category 10. Don't ever allow your problem to persist on your level. Your problem is not on your level. If your problem dwells on your same level, then you've demoted yourself and promoted your issue and that's a problem.

Like an eagle, in the eye of the storm rise above it and use the winds to elevate your faith to new dimensions. An eagle understands the importance of the winds and uses them to his advantage. He stretches out his wings and rides it out. Whatever winds are blowing in your life, take advantage of the situation and ride it out. Don't give up, ride it out! Don't allow the adversity to take advantage of you,

you take advantage of it. Take charge and turn your greatest opposition into a humongous opportunity to ascend to a height you've never gone. Watch your faith escalate to a higher place and your life successfully soar to another realm. You got this! The winds may beat you upside the head, but the winds can't beat your faith. Your faith has the power to beat your storm. Now tell the devil, doubt and unbelief to beat it!

In Acts 27, the Apostle Paul is being extradited to Rome to make an appeal before Caesar because his appointed time had come. At that time in the text, he is in prison for a crime he didn't commit and must make a plea for his release. Paul and other prisoners are placed on a ship and while being transported their ship was hit with a storm. The storm was not an introductory Category 1 Storm. It was equivalent to a Level 5 and was out to kill. Acts 27:14 describes the wind. The scripture says, *"But not long after there arose against it a tempestuous wind, called Euroclydon."* The word "arose" means to give over into one's care or to entrust one with something. The troublesome wind "arose" because God could trust

Paul with trouble. Can God trust you with trouble? Absolutely! God allowed some treacherous things to rise up against you because He could trust you with it. He placed your storm under your care because He trusts you. It's not above you, it's under you. That's why you can't be careless with it because it's been assigned to your care. You are responsible for seeing it through and God is liable for seeing you through it.

The wind that manifested during the prisoner's voyage is "called" Euroclydon which is a typhonic wind or a typhoon. Anything that is "called" has a "call" and anything with a "call" has a purpose. This wind had a purpose and that was to violently devour and destroy. A typhoon is a whirlwind personified as a giant and accredited to being the father of winds. This giant was determined to slay and demolish everything and everyone that was in its path. It was coming strong and was unstoppable in its approach. The winds and the waves possessed the nature of a typhonic maniac and were so violent that they caused the ship to break. Lord Jesus! Acts 27:41 tells us that the hinder part of the ship was struck and began to break because of the violence of the waves. Though the attack was ferocious, God still granted Apostle Paul victory in the midst of the violence. What a mighty God we serve!

When storms move in your direction, they do not operate in a passive manner; therefore you must never be passive in your faith by operating in fear. Passive Faith is Aggressive Fear. Fear will forcefully give the storm permission to have its way in your life and authorize the winds to wipe you utterly out. During the trials of life your faith must stretch forth its hand, reach into the Word of the Lord and lay hold of the promises of God. You must firmly stand in the volume of the book and know that the Lord will not let you fail neither will He allow you to fall. Embrace peace and command peace to be still.

POWERPOINT

**Passive Faith is Aggressive Fear.**

God is faithful and will give you peace through the storm as you stand on His infallible Word. He will give you perfect peace if you keep your mind stayed on Him. Not on what's happening around you, but fixed on Him who is with you. The winds and the storms of life can only do to you what God allows. Nahum 1:3 tells us, *"...the Lord hath his way in the whirlwind and in the storm, and the clouds are the dust of his feet."* No matter what you go through the Lord is going have His way and God is going to the get the glory. In fact, He is going to use your storm to do it. As the scripture declares, the Lord will have His way "in" the whirlwind and "in" the storm. In order to have His way "in" it, He has to get "in" it. Move out of the way, rest your mind and don't be troubled in your spirit because God is getting ready to get "in" the storm with you. Let Him have His way. Tell him, *"Lord have your way in my life, have your way in my struggle, have your way in my adversity. These gigantic winds are blowing strong, but have your way. The storm seems so unbearable, so have your way. I trust you Lord and I know you won't leave me out here to die like this. Get in this fight with me and have your way."*

The fight is great, but the God we serve is Greater. His name is El HaGadol. He's a Great, Huge, Large, Big, and Enormous God. There's nothing or nobody greater. He's so great that even His name is great and greatly to be praised. It doesn't matter how big your problem is. What matters most is how big your God is. El HaGadol is much bigger and far greater. Greater is He that is in you, than the very thing that has come against you. No matter how enormous your struggle is, you were destined to overcome it. You have victory in your DNA and you have triumph flowing through your bloodstream. You were built to last and born to win. There's a winner in you that will evict the whiner out of you. Don't whine about it; just get ready to shine in it. Don't ever allow your whine to take away your shine. Shift out of that dark place and shine the like the Sun (indicative of the Son). When the Sun shines, it's a sign that it's almost your time – time for the storm to come to a complete end and for you to land on your new beginning.

You can't lose so count it all joy and allow the joy of the Lord to be your strength to make it through your worse season. The ship may break, but don't you break. You have to make it and I need you to survive the storm. You have more power than you really know therefore rise up in strength. When you are weak, at that very moment, He is strong. Weakness is an opportunity for God to reveal His strength. Ask the Lord to give you Ischus Power. Ischus is a Greek word that denotes one's ability, force, strength and might. It's simply Power to Do! Do what? Whatever needs to be done. Ischus Power gives you supernatural ability to do what you could not do before. It grants you the confidence that you can do ALL THINGS through Christ who strengthens you.

Ischus Power is a *"Philippians 4:13 Grace"* that provides you with favour to do what ordinarily seems impossible to get done. It transforms the possibility of impossibilities into great possibilities. You can do all things. You can survive the storm, you can conquer the winds and like the Apostle Paul, you can make it out on broken pieces. Yes, the ship may have broken but thank God that He left you with the broken pieces to swim your way out. You didn't die in it therefore, praise God for it. You survived and you shall overcome.

# CHAPTER 2

*Mastering Your Emotions In Times of Crisis*

# MASTERING YOUR EMOTIONS IN TIMES OF CRISIS

I've studied Roman culture especially as it relates to warfare and battle. In fights between opponents, the objective of those contending is to go after its rival's head. Reason being is that whoever had the head had the victory. In Roman warfare and wrestling, antagonists would endeavor to attack its victim's head, crush their windpipe and gauge out their challenger's eyes. This type of attack left the opponent in a state of defeat and in many cases death. Whoever had the head, had the victory. 1 Samuel 17 allows us to witness David's conquest over Goliath.

In 1 Samuel 17:46 David declares to Goliath that he is going to take his head off. He says, *"This day will the LORD deliver thee into mine hand; and I will smite thee, and take thine head from thee..."* The warrior in David embraced the fact that whoever lays hold of the head has the victory. Ultimate triumph was not in David bringing Goliath down, but total victory was achieved when David cut Goliath's head off. Again, whoever has the head has the victory. The awesomeness of David's triumph is that David used Goliath's sword to take his head. When you have your head together in battle, God will allow you to use your enemy's weapon to slay your enemy and take his head off.

In times of great warfare, it is crucial that you keep your head together. Before you can apprehend your enemy's head, you must make certain you have your head on straight. Your mind must be sharp and your discernment must be keen. You must maintain mental clarity and emotional stability. Whatever you do, don't lose it. The condition of your head is what will determine if you get ahead in life and successfully move beyond setbacks and fatal blowbacks. You must think forward in order to move forward. Never allow your feelings to permit opposing circumstances to push you backward. You must think and feel your way forward. The condition of a person's head dominates a person's feelings. Your emotions are influenced by what and how you think. Apostle Paul, who experienced shipwreck in Acts 27, proclaims in Acts 26:2 that he had to think himself happy while being faced with a great challenge. He was giving his thoughts permission to dictate his emotions. When you are faced with fires and floods, you must properly manage your emotions. Your soul must be anchored in the Lord. Hebrews 6:19 describes an anchor as this: *"It's an unbreakable spiritual lifeline, reaching past all appearances right to the very presence of God."* – Message Bible

When you allow Jesus to be the Anchor of your soul, He becomes your unbreakable spiritual lifeline so that no matter what you go through your soul does not break. When your soul (your mind, your will, your emotions and your intellect) is stable in Christ, it is impossible for you to have a nervous breakdown. Instead, you walk in mighty breakthrough. The Lord will keep you and uphold you with the right hand of His righteousness. You don't have to fear or be dismayed. You can rest your mind in the fact that He is your Lifeline that will keep you from drowning in the raging sea. In a state of emergency not only will

He be your Lifeline, He will also be your Life Guard. When it looks like the waves of life are overtaking you, He will swim to your rescue when you cry for help.

When Paul was in the midst of the storm, initially he lost control emotionally and began to speak negatively. Negative words are birthed out of negative emotions which are conceived in the womb of a negative mind which perceived that the situation's outcome was negative. The winds were divergent, sailing was dangerous and the circumstance looked extremely deleterious. Paul allowed fear and panic to temporarily influence his emotions and taint his perception. He authorized adversity to provoke him to speak negatively. He uttered forth out of his mouth these words in Acts 27:10, *"And he said unto them, Sirs, I perceive that this voyage will be with hurt and much damage, not only of the lading and ship, but also of our lives."* Notice Paul says he perceives, which describes the state of his perception.

P✹WERP✹INT

**You must think forward in order to move forward. Never allow your feelings to permit opposing circumstances to push you backward.**

The storm had affected Paul's emotions and began to poison his belief. Paul started speaking off because he perceived off. He perceives and proclaims that their voyage will be with hurt and much damage. At that very moment, his negative words caused their situation to become more negative. There is death and life in the power of the tongue. Paul spoke destruction into the atmosphere therefore, the spirit of destruction obtained liberty to begin to destruct.

It is vital that you rule your mind and guard your mouth when faced with calamity. There is a protocol that I practice that I call the *Mind, Mouth, Manifestation Principle*. When you think it in your mind, then you speak it out of your mouth, it will manifest in your life. You shall have whatever you say. If you speak death, you will see death. If you speak life, you will have life. God always puts before us life and death and He tells us to choose life. When our emotions are out of control, the insanity that operates in us chooses death. Fear seduced the man of God, Apostle Paul, into speaking a death sentence into existence. Exactly four verses after negativity departed from his mouth, disaster entered into their lives. Matters got worse and immediately Euroclydon manifested. This typhonic hurricane came out of nowhere, or shall I say out of Paul's mouth. Paul was losing it emotionally and he became frantic mentally. He was in need of some serious courage because it looked like he was getting ready to die. He was in a state of emergency and needed supernatural strength and chivalry to make it out. Something was robbing him of his tenacity to endure and draining him of his courage to go on. What was it? The answer is revealed in Acts 27:24. The bible declares that the Angel of God came and stood by him in the night and spoke to him, "*Saying, Fear not, Paul; thou must be brought before Caesar: and, lo, God hath given thee all them that sail with thee.*" The first thing the Angel addresses to Paul is fear. He commands him to fear not. Fear is the spirit that was ruling his emotions and depriving him of his bravery. Paul allowed the spirit of fear to enter in. He had mismanaged his emotions and al-

P⬡WERP⬡INT

**Negative words are birthed out of negative emotions which are conceived in the womb of a negative mind which perceived that the situation's outcome was negative.**

lowed fear to take control. At that very moment this spirit began to dominate his thoughts, affect his feelings and speak through his mouth. The spirit of fear spoke evil out of him and more evil rose up against him.

You can't afford to mismanage your words because of not properly mastering your emotions. If your emotions are jacked up, your life will be jacked up. It's best to be quiet and hear what God is saying. During great adversity, we must yield our ears and our mouth to the Holy Spirit. We must resist allowing fear to talk us out our faith because without faith things can become extremely fatal. Our ear must be inclined to hear the voice of the Lord. During perils and distresses, it is vital that we tune into heavens frequency and turn up the volume on the Word of the Lord. It's imperative that while going through the storms of life and the winds are roaring boisterously that you allow the Word to out talk the Wind. Speak the Word of God over the wind and allow your faith to silence your fears. Your faith will shift your emotions back into alignment in order for you to mentally move forward.

As we persist in the text we see by verse 22 that Apostle Paul shifts mentally and rearranges some things emotionally. He captures his contrary words and cancels them in the atmosphere. He speaks life to swallow up the power of death. He then prophetically proclaims in Acts 17:22, *"And now I exhort you to be of good cheer: for there shall be no loss of any man's life among you, but of the ship."* Paul couldn't exhort them THEN, but he says, "And NOW I exhort you." Now that he had his emotions subjected, his soul anchored, his heart strengthened and his mind encouraged, he could NOW exhort others that were going through the storm also.

It's hard to exhort others when your vision of victory is distorted. The Angel of God showed up to strengthen and empower the man of God to see his victory in the midst of a vicious storm. Often times when we get in trouble, our emotions are also in trouble which leads to even more trouble. A tumultuous emotional life can be the root cause of a disastrous life. It's during times of soulish distress that we are to call on the Lord to be our Jehovah Ezer. Jehovah Ezer is one of God's names and means He is my

Help. The Lord is faithful and will be our very present help in the time of trouble. It's our trouble that qualifies us for immediate assistance. A present help is the kind of help that has to show up NOW. The present is not later, but it's now. Now is instantly, immediately, rapidly and suddenly. Trouble provokes the immediately and invokes God to do something NOW. Now unto Him who is able to do exceeding abundantly above all we can ask or think according to the power that works within us. God wants to do something extraordinary for you NOW, but He will only do it according to the power that works in you. In order for the miraculous to be done, the power in you has to work even in the midst of a mess. Keep your head together. Don't allow yourself to have an emotional power outage. Your power has to work.

The power that Ephesian 3:20 is speaking of is called Dunamis Power. It is power for performing miracles and more importantly it is mental power or what I call "Think Power." The miracle that God is waiting to perform is going to be accomplished through the mental power or "Think Power" that you possess. Be strengthened in your mind. Be empowered in your emotions. When you think right, everything will turn out alright. Anoint your head with oil, speak peace over your mind and rest to your soul. Don't worry about what is going on in your life, but instead pray about it. God will do the exceeding abundantly above all you can ask or think. You simply have to give him a powerful thought to work with and He will do above and beyond what you thought. Your thoughts alone will release the power to change your situation and help you in overcoming life's struggles.

P❋WERP❋INT

**It's hard to exhort others when your vision of victory is distorted.**

Master the system of your soul. Clean out the archives of your emotions. Give the womb of your mind a mental DNC. Cultivate your perception, consecrate your mentality and prepare yourself for supernatural conception. God wants to get your thought life pregnant and get you ready to birth something real good in a real bad situation. Tell your soul to say yes to whatever God is doing in your life. Cancel the assignment of depression, cast off the spirit of fear and put on the garment of praise for the spirit of heaviness. God's going to turn your mourning into dancing. Your weeping only endures for a night, but joy comes in the morning. Make a conscious decision that you are going to bless the Lord at all times and allow His praises to continually be in your mouth. Command your soul to make her boast in the Lord and the humble shall hear thereof and be glad. Let your testimony be this, *"I sought the Lord and He heard me and delivered me from all my fears."* God has not given you the spirit of fear, but of power and of love and of a sound mind.

------

P❂WERP❂INT

**A tumultuous emotional life can be the root cause of a disastrous life.**

Declare that you have a sound mind and your ears will hear the sound of Victory and Triumph. When the Children of Israel were at the wall of Jericho, they had a sound mind and that's why they were able to hear a sound and produce a sound. Their deliverance was in the sound. Their breakthrough was in the sound. It was the sound that caused the wall to fall flat. When you have a sound mind and a sound mouth, every force of opposition will have to bow and every wall will have to come tumbling down. When the forces against you come down, the Lord is going to take you up. When you go up, the Lord is going to take you up in a shout. Shout your way up and praise your way out! You are destined to win and born to overcome. Clap your hands all ye people and shout unto God with a voice of triumph (Psalm 47:1). If the enemy can take away your voice, then he robs you of the victory. You are the voice of victory.

You must keep your head up because your body follows your head. If your head is down, you will be down. If your head is up, then you will go up. Your body will move in the direction of your head. Your feet doesn't follow your hands, your feet follows your head. The head is the head and the head leads. Heads of families lead. Heads of companies lead. Heads of government lead. Your life follows the direction of your head. When the Children of Israel were in the valley of Jericho and had to climb the hills to get to Jerusalem, they said I will lift up mine eyes unto the hills from whence comest my help and all of my help comes from the Lord. When their head lifted, their eyes lifted because you can't lift your eyes without lifting your head. So lift up your head oh ye gates and be ye lifted up ye everlasting doors and the King of Glory will come in. He will come into your struggle and give you divine strength so that you can make it out on broken pieces.

# CHAPTER 3

*There's Purpose Behind My Pain*

# There's Purpose Behind My Pain

I remember the day that I had my daughter, my first child. My pregnancy was very rough. My daughter was very large and her size was quite enormous. At birth, she weighed 9 pounds and 6 ounces. On the day of delivery the pain was so great. It was the worst pain that I had ever experienced in my entire life. My contractions were excruciating and the labor pains were brutal. I felt like my insides were going to collapse. I screamed and yelled. Kicked and hollered. I was losing control of myself and thought that I was going to lose my mind because the pain was so intense. I cried with a loud voice and asked the nurse why the pain was so great. I felt traumatized. The nurse replied and said, *"Your contractions are so sharp, aggressive and much needed because of the size of your baby."* She went on to say that the pain from the contractions would be the thing that would give me the power to push.  On that delivery table I realized the power of pain.  The greater the pain; the greater the

P❋WERP❋INT

**The size of your pain often times describes the size of your purpose and the weight of your promise.**

push.  The size of your pain often times describes the size of your purpose and the weight of your promise.  Without the pain, you wouldn't have the power to push.  I got up in the strength of my pain and used it to my fullest potential until my pain caused me to gain.  Every time I pushed it hurt but after all the pain, the hurt was the thing that really helped.  It helped me to bring forth my baby girl.

You can't produce anything great in the earth without pain.  All pain has a purpose.  The bible says in Isaiah 66:8 that as soon as Zion travailed she brought forth.  One of the meanings of travail means to go through torture.  God can use our torture to help bring forth our treasure.  There's purpose behind your pain.  There are many scriptures in the bible that reveal pain's purpose and benefits of bad.  Exodus 1:12 is a great witness that testifies of the blessings associated with pain.  This scripture says, *"But the more they afflicted them, the more they multiplied and grew.  And they were grieved because of the children of Israel."*  The Hebrew word for affliction is Anah.  Anah means to be put down, to weaken, to browbeat and to cause trouble.  Though the enemy afflicted Israel, the more they multiplied and grew.  Their adversaries thought that the trouble they caused them would set them back, however the affliction set them up.  The afflicted reaped a two-fold blessing.  They multiplied and they grew.  God knows how to give us double for our trouble.

There is purpose behind your pain and your disaster has definition, a meaning yet to be told. Webster's dictionary cut some things out of your pain's meaning.  He didn't totally describe the full meaning of your disaster.  His definition was watered down and didn't carry enough weight.  You have to provide your own definition to define the struggles that you've gone through.  You must create your own dictionary to define your own devastation.  I'd like to give my personal definition of my pain from the

Williams Dictionary. Now the dictionary according to dictionary.com describes pain as physical suffering or distress, as due to injury or illness. It further mentions that pain is mental or emotional suffering or torment. I partly agree with this definition; however it's leaving some crucial ingredients out. According to my dictionary pain is defined as this:

*Pain is God's purpose to prosper me and the devil's plan to destroy me. It is the element that God chooses to use to cause multiplication and growth to take place my life. It is the pathway that leads me to an avenue of abundance and overwhelming prosperity. Pain is a prerequisite for promotion. Its effects have me feeling discouraged and demoted, but it unlocks my potential which gives me the courage to walk in my promotion. Pain is like a 2 edged sword; it's my greatest hurt that helped me up higher to a place called Greater. – The Williams Dictionary*

The Lord purposes for us to prosper through pain. Great multiplication and growth should take place after great affliction. The children of God were blessed as a result of all the bad they experienced. The more they were afflicted the more they grew and multiplied. More Pain means More Gain! God is setting you up for something so awesome, mighty and great. Multiplication in Exodus 1:12 means to become great, to become much, to do much, to make large, to enlarge, and to increase greatly or exceedingly. Out of the womb of grief is coming forth your greatness. God is enlarging you, blessing you and making you great. Your pain is taking your little and turning it and you into much. You are becoming much and you will do much so don't be surprised when people start calling you suchy-much. You are all that and your pain and affliction helped you to become it! Thank God for your pain, it's serving its purpose.

The second benefit of the Children of Israel's pain was to grow them. Not only did they multiply, but they grew. The word Grew in the scripture means to break through, to break down, to break away, to break forth and to burst open. More specifically it's to break over limitations and to burst open, burst out and burst forth into increase. If you've suffered from hurt and pain, you ought to get excited because something good is coming out of it. You shall break through every barrier. You shall break down every wall in your way. You shall break away from the hold of your enemy. God is breaking the arm of your Pharaoh. You are going to break forth into great abundance and burst open hidden treasures out of dark places.

Look at the purpose of God over the plan of the enemy. In the above mentioned verse, the children of the Lord were afflicted by the Egyptians and in bondage in the land of Egypt. The Egyptian system was very binding and limited God's people in a major way. God used pain to prosper them and affliction to free them. While bound by limitations, their affliction was the very thing that God allowed to break them beyond all limitations, barriers and bondages that had constrained them for years. They were put down and minimized but in the end they broke forth and were maximized. When you're full of pain, that's when God is trying to maximize you to your fullest potential. Your pain is bringing great potential out of you. Potential is hidden power assigned to a person to accomplish a specific purpose. Your pain validates that you have purpose. The reason why you were hurt is because the Lord purposes to raise you up to a tremendous height. Hurt is helping you up higher. You've been put down long enough. The devil may have even told you that you were never going to be nothing and that's because he knows that you are something and somebody extraordinarily great. The enemy is threatened by you and is really terrified of you. He's afraid that if you ever find out whom you really are in God, that it is over! He knows if you rise in power, that his power to manipulate, control, dominate and limit your life is completely broken. He knows that if you ever allow God to blow you up that you will blow him away. Brace yourself, because you are the BOMB that's about to BLOW up! BOOM! A "Boom Experience" is an encounter that causes you to experience rapid growth, sudden increase, accelerated progress and abundant prosperity. You are highly explosive and about to flourish vigorously. Get ready because the Lord is going to blow you up. Boom!

The theme of this book is built upon the hard-

ship of the Apostle Paul, a prisoner of Christ, in Acts 27. This
man of God suffered from so
much pain and was opposed by
numerous challenges. His pain
most definitely had an incredi-

ble purpose. I previously mentioned to you that Paul
and the other prisoners were attacked by a typhonic
wind called Euroclydon. This wind was also known
as a North Easter Wind. This wind is the same wind
that comes to separate the wheat from the tare. Tare
is counterfeit wheat who purposes to overtake and
destroy wheat by choking it out. There must be a
separation lest there be an assassination. Wrong as-
sociations can be the cause of your annihilation.

When God is separating you for a greater purpose, He will allow a wind to hit your life that He
might remove certain people and things out of your
life. Winds are not necessarily designed to destroy
you, but rather consecrate you and separate you that
you may be fit for the Master's use. If you are ever
going to become a Masterpiece, you must undergo
your process of separation. God has to separate you

so that you can stand out above the rest. Masterpieces stand out. They are separated, elevated and put on public display. Before God can display you, He has to detach the tare from you. Tare desires to GROW with you, however they're not ordained to GO with you. According to Matthew 13:30, the wheat and the tare grew together then the wind came because it was not God's plan for them to go together. As God grows you, there are some people that just can't go with you. As God elevates you, it's the wind that will remove Tare People out of your life.

Let's take some time to identify the tare in your life. First of all, tare resembles wheat. It looks just like it (on the surface). Its appearance can be quite deceiving, if you don't have an eye to discern it. Tare People are deceptive people that want to look like you, desire to be you, and will try to kill you because you are you. Oh my God! If the tare continues to grow with the wheat, ultimately the tare ends up choking out the wheat. Tare People are deceptive and the only reason they are still around you is to eventually choke you, strangle you and try to destroy you. Their motives are impure and their desires are deadly. On the outside tare looks like wheat, but at the core its grains are black. Black represents death and destruction. At the root, tare is out to kill, steal and destroy.

Wind actually reveals tare amongst wheat. When the wind blows, wheat bows but tare will not bend. The wind provokes wheat to bow to the presence and power of God. Wind will draw worship out of wheat and will build bitterness in tare.

---

P❀WERP❀INT

**Tare People are deceptive people that want to look like you, desire to be you, and will try to kill you because you are you.**

Wheat People worship their way through storms and praise their way out of trouble. Tare People become bitter and blame God when they encounter life's bad. Storms make Tare People bitter and it makes Wheat People better.

Tare is usually separated from wheat at harvest time. When God allow Euroclydon Winds to sweep through your life, it's a sign that it's Harvest Time. Remember, the wind causes a separation of the wheat and the tare and the separation comes during the harvest. You've been attacked by so many winds, but rejoice because it's Harvest Time. When God purposes for you to walk into your Season of Harvest, everybody can't go. God must remove the tare. They may have grown with you, but they can't go with you. They can't go with you on this next level. It's not that you have to dislike them or hate them, they just can't go. They won't be able to walk with you on this next dimension. They are like rocket boosters in that they must fall off. They simply were not designed to fly in your airspace. So

P ❋ WERP ❋ INT

**Stop worrying about the people (the tare) that are no longer with you, get excited about where God is taking you.**

when they're no longer with you and it seems as if though they left you, just know that it was God that removed them. Tare can only remain with wheat for a season, but when your season shifts the tare has to go. Stop worrying about the people (the tare) that are no longer with you, get excited about where God is taking you. You're going up. It's Harvest Time. Your season is upon you and a greater blessing is getting ready to be released to you!

# CHAPTER 4

## I'm Anointed For This

# I'm Anointed For This

God will never allow you to go through anything without making the anointing available to you to get through it. The anointing is supernatural ability to do what you cannot do by yourself and to do what you could not do before. God always anoints people to accomplish purposes. Without a purpose, there is no need for the anointing. The anointing provides us with the ability to achieve great things in the earth. It is very important that every believer is anointed. It is a special endowment for special people to accomplish special things. The anointing is so necessary that even Jesus himself was anointed. He was anointed to preach glad tidings and proclaim good news. Isaiah 61:1 says, *"The Spirit of the Lord God is upon me, because the Lord has anointed and qualified me to preach the Gospel of good tidings to the meek, the poor, and afflicted; He has sent me to bind up and heal the brokenhearted, to proclaim liberty to the [physical and spiritual] captives and the opening of the prison and of the eyes to those who are bound."* – Amplified Bible

The anointing qualifies you to successfully and victoriously overcome your storms. God anoints those that He can trust with trouble. Why? It's because the anointing produces an uncommon ability to overcome uncommon challenges. This uncommon ability also produces an uncommon strength to break through uncommon struggles and achieve uncommon results. This ability is supernatural and makes us more than able. Not just able, but more than able to do. Anointed people have an "I Can Do Spirit." They are fully persuaded that they can do all things through Christ that strengthens them. They can because they are qualified. God Himself has qualified you for the battle you're facing right now. You have been hired for the position and because you've been anointed for it, promotion is the inevitable.

In 1 Samuel 16, the prophet Samuel arrives at Jesse's house to anoint one of Jesse's sons to become the next King of Israel. There are eight sons and seven of them didn't qualify. It was the eighth son who qualified for the anointing and was approved by God to one day be the King of Israel. His name is David, which means the Beloved of God. We are now God's beloved and very special and precious to Him. Like David, we are rare, unique, uncommon and unusual. When God places an anointing on an unusual person, He will allow them to face unusual challenges for the purpose of achieving unusual victories. When you're anointed, your struggle is not like everybody else's. The hell you go through is absolutely insane and will leave you confused about why the fight against you is so great. If you don't know the degree of your anointing, then you will be bewildered about the intensity of your battle. The demons that you have to fight are great in number because of the greatness of the anointing that is on your life. The devil knows who you are and realizes that you've been anointed for this. THIS is that thing that is trying to shake you up and break you down. THIS is your difficulty that is trying to cause your delay. THIS is that sickness that the devil said was unto death. THIS is that financial burden that is trying to bankrupt your soul. You're anointed for THIS.

What you go through is out of the ordinary because you're extraordinary. Extraordinary people have EXTRA. You have been given extra strength, extra stamina, extra endurance and most of all extra oil, the anointing. The anointing gives you divine permission to live in the EXTRA. Now because you are endowed with extra, you are equipped to take what the average person can't. That's why God allows you to go through because He knows you can handle it. You're anointed for this. You have the ability to defeat what would defeat others. You are more than able to conquer the demons and demonic forces that would conquer others. The devil Himself knows who you are and the anointing that you possess. You just have to know it and confidently walk in it.

As we continue to examine David in 1 Samuel 16, we see that he receives an anointing to be king. As time progresses, later by 2 Samuel 2:4 we see that he receives his appointing to be king. Between David's anointing and appointing he has to go through hell, but the anointing qualifies him to make it out. Whatever you are going through, come hell or high-water, you are qualified to overcome. You will not be delayed neither will you be denied; you're qualified.

1 Samuel 30 is a transitional season in David's life and a very pivotal period in time. He has literally graced a Destiny Moment. This Destiny Moment is a Redefining Moment and is accompanied by great misery. David is closer to his destiny than he's ever been before. The chapter opens by saying, "And it came to pass." The phrase "And it came to pass" denotes the fulfillment of a prophetic promise. The place that David's prophecy begins to come to pass is at a place called Ziklag. At Ziklag, David suffered extreme misery; however he had graced his moment. Your pain is a clue that you are real close to your prophecy and your misery validates that you have approached a tremendous moment.

P✺WERP✺INT

**Your pain is a clue that you are real close to your prophecy and your misery validates that you have approached a tremendous moment.**

When David was at Ziklag, the Amalekites burned the place down with fire. David is going through one of the worse Hell's that he had every gone through. These enemies burned the city, laid hold of his possessions, stole his stuff and had taken his family into captivity. Major devastation manifested in David's life. Ziklag in Hebrew means to spiral down. It looked like David was going down real quick, but he qualified to survive. He was opposed by a temporary setback, but his comeback was greater than his setback. David was weary and weak. He cried until he had no more power to weep, but he had to make an instant decision that he was going to get his bounce back. His destiny was on the line.

Right before major Destiny Moments, we are often opposed by great misery. Misfortune and misery precedes Destiny Moments. Misfortune is a clue that something magnificent is fortunately getting ready to happen immediately after you endure great misery. The devil would love to get you caught up on the misery, but keep your eyes on your destiny and know that what's to come is better than what's been. Don't become distracted by the pain. There is

**Misfortune is a clue that something magnificent is fortunately getting ready to happen immediately after you endure great misery.**

destiny after your devastation. You're not hurting for nothing and neither is your pain in vain. God will not waste your suffering. God sees your tears. David cried until he had no more power to weep. He was literally tired of crying. He was surrounded by devastation, but he was extremely close to his destiny.

Destiny is what God has predestined and predetermined to take place before the foundations of the world. Destiny was presupposed before inception and already established in the heavens prior to your conception. David's destiny housed the fulfillment of the prophetic word that the Prophet Samuel declared over him regarding becoming the next King. Destiny is the place where your prophecy has already come to pass. That's why 1 Samuel 30 opens by declaring, "And it came to pass." The prophecy came to pass at Ziklag. Though Ziklag was a painful place, it also was a prophetic birthing place. David was running from his past, but was still pregnant with his future. A king was about to be born. His water was about to break. Water puts out fires. The water of his womb was getting ready to cause the fire to cease and David was about to get his release. When your pain collides with your prophecy, God will launch you into your destiny. David cried and cried, but the cry of his destiny was louder than the cry of his pain and for that cause God birthed forth his prophecy.

David was hurting so bad and needed an immediate shift. A shift is when you are transitioned from one place to another swiftly. A shift is when something that is lowercase is made uppercase, when little is turned into much and when very small is made enormously big. Though things were extremely bad, God was using all the bad to make him bigger. Not only was David about to get bigger, everything was about to get better. There is a major shift that's happening in your life. You cannot stay where you are. A destiny shift is taking place. You are about to go from

---

**P❂WERP❂INT**

**When your pain collides with your prophecy, God will launch you into your destiny.**

here to there, just like that. This shift is going to be quick. Divine acceleration will be released so that your transition into what's next will happen swiftly. What would have taken years to accomplish is going to happen in a day. A day unto the Lord is as a thousand years and a thousand years is like a day (2 Peter 3:8). A thousand years of waiting is shifting into one day of reaping. God is shifting you into what's next and He's doing it right now. You're on the verge of a phenomenal Destiny Shift!

The bible says in 1 Samuel 30 that David encouraged himself in the Lord. The Hebrew word for encouraged is Chazaq which means to praise yourself into the victory. You are one praise away from the victory. You are one shout away from your breakthrough. You've been through so much and all you got left is your praise. David made a decision to turn his pain into praise. You have a praise locked up on the inside of you waiting to come forth.

---

P✺WERP✺INT

**The Hebrew word for encouraged is Chazaq which means to praise yourself into the victory.**

When praise emerges out of your pain, God will use

your pain to launch you into your prophetic destiny. Sometimes the only way to get out of what was and enter into what's to come is to praise your way out and praise your way in. When David praised, He unlocked his destiny. God wants to give you the Key of David and praise is the key. Praise will open up the atmosphere of your future and shut the door on the devastations of the past. Praise will shift you out of defeat and shoot you forth into mighty victory.

Secondly, the word encouraged in Hebrew also means to loose oneself. David was tied up mentally and he was bound emotionally. Things had been confiscated physically and he was robbed economically. He needed to be liberated and set free. He had no one else to loose him; therefore, he had to loose himself. Life's difficulties have a way of binding you up. Fires, frustration, worry, stress, anxiety, heartache and pain all have a way of imprisoning your soul and blocking you from reaching your destiny. Discouragement binds but encouragement looses. When David encouraged himself, a loosing on the earth took place. When there is a loosing on the earth, there also has to be a loosing in Heaven. This biblical principle and protocol is established in Matthew 18:18. The Word of the Lord declares, *"Verily I say unto you, Whatsoever ye shall bind on earth shall be bound in heaven: and whatsoever ye shall loose on earth shall be loosed in heaven."* Whoever David was in Heaven had to be loosed the very moment he loosed himself on the earth. David was a King in Heaven. Heaven is the place where prophecy originates and the prophetic futuristic us exists. When the Devastated David got loosed at Ziklag, the *Prophetic David* got loosed in Heaven. When you praise God in the midst of your pain, your praise will loose you into your prophecy and usher you into your destiny.

Everything that you have been through was never for your destruction, but it was for the purpose of getting you to your destiny. The devastation that you experienced was actually destiny in disguise. I know you couldn't see it while going through your Ziklag Experience. The fire was intense and the smoke was thick. The smoke almost blinded you, but after the smoke clears you will see everything that God has purposed for you. It will surely come to pass. When overwhelmed by life threatening situations, you can't always see what God is doing. You just have to know that He's working. He's not a man that He should lie, neither the Son of Man that He should repent. Whatever He promised you, He is faithful to perform.

Like David, the fire almost killed you and like Apostle Paul, the storm almost destroyed you, but that the Lord has anointed you. You have been anointed to survive your Ziklag. Not only will you survive, but God will restore. You are going to get back everything that you have lost and more. You shall recover all. The anointing of the Holy Spirit qualifies you to come out hell and walk in your heavenly promises then see the manifestation of your prophecy. Whoever you are in Heaven, get ready because you are about to become it on Earth. God is using your pain as a stepping stone into your promotion. At Ziklag you were spiraling down, but God has purposed to raise you up. You're getting up from that place and you're about to walk in another dimension of grace. The Lord is alleviating you from all the pressure and launching you into divine promotion. Your past can't hold you and where you are can't keep you. You've been anointed for a time such as this. Destiny is calling you and the cry of your destiny is louder than the cry of your devastation. There is a cry in the Spirit. Destiny is calling you to be free. This cry drowns out the sound of your pain because it carries the sound of your purpose. The cry emanates from within and reminds you that you're coming out.

You qualify. You've been anointed for this. God has anointed your head with oil and now your cup shall run over. The adversary of your soul attempted to take you under and for that cause the blessings of the Lord shall run over. The blessing of the Lord is going to make you rich and add no sorrow with it (Proverbs 10:22). Today you are released from the pain and have been given divine permission to prosper. Be free in Jesus name. Sing the song of the Lord and proclaim, *"I am free. Praise the Lord, I'm free. No longer bound, no more chains holding me. My soul is resting and it's just another blessing, Praise the Lord Hallelujah, I'm free."* You're anointed to be free. Be free from the yoke oppression, depression and rejection. The anointing destroys every yoke. The yoke of bondage that is binding you to your past pain and hindering you from advancing into your future promise is being destroyed.

The anointing is healing you and making you whole. The anointing is made of five compound ingredients. Authentic anointing oil in the days of Moses as described in Exodus 30:22-25 included: Cinnamon, Calamus, Cassia, Olive Oil and Myrrh. All these ingredients assisted in healing the wounded and in restoring the injured. Each ingredient has a natural purpose and holds spiritual significance. In each element of the anointing there is a specific remedy that will help in surviving trauma and being relieved from pain.

# INGREDIENTS FOR THE AUTHENTIC ANOINTING OIL

## Cinnamon

Cinnamon is an old ancient remedy, prescribed for everything from diarrhea, nausea, to influenza and parasitic worms. More specifically it is prescribed for chills. This remedy can also help people with cold feet and hands, especially at night. The smell of Cinnamon is pleasant, stimulates the senses and yet calms the nerves.

*The anointing will keep you calm
even in the midst of calamity.*

SWEETFLAG
*Acorus calamus L.*
ARUM FAMILY

# Calamus

C alamus has been used for centuries as an anesthetic, which helps you lose sensation without losing consciousness. Calamus has been historically used as a remedy for headaches and toothaches. It helps maintain mental focus as well as helps increase endurance and stamina.

*The anointing will relieve your headache that came with the heartache. It will allow you to maintain mental focus so that your pain and suffering won't become a distraction.*

# Cassia

C assia is similar to Cinnamon but greater in strength and quality. Cassia is a stimulant that strengthens the action of the heart so that those who were wounded and had an injured heart would not faint.

*The anointing will give power to the faint and increase strength in them that have no might (Isaiah 40:29).*

Cassia also helps prevent Epilepsy and seizures. Epilepsy is a brain disorder in which abnormal bursts of electrical activity occur in cells of the brain, resulting in seizures. When one was wounded, a blow to the head in the beating could have caused a seizure or spasmodic convulsion. Cassia was used to avert the onset of epileptic breakdown.

*The anointing will keep your brain fully functioning and operating at its fullest potential during times of severe crisis.*

## Olive Oil

Olive Oil helps to clean abrasions, cuts and wounds, relieves aching muscles. It is known to have an anti-inflammatory agent in it which fits infections and irritation. Olive oil causes healing to take place quickly.

*The anointing will clean off all residue from your old injuries in war and wipe off the blood still on you from every previous battle. In addition, your healing will be quick because of the anointing.*

## Myrrh

**M**yrrh was a very expensive ingredient. It was one of the three gifts that the three Wise Men brought to Jesus.

*The anointing isn't cheap. It will cost you something. You must be willing to pay the price to possess it.*

Myrrh is used as a remedy for hard to heal wounds.

*The anointing will heal those wounds that you never thought could be healed.*

Myrrh actually means bitter. To be bitter is having a harsh, disagreeably acrid taste.

*Bitterness is disagreeable to the taste. God allows a hint of bitterness in your oil to remind you that though you disagree with the things you've been through and the pain you've suffered, that because of it you're a thousand times better. Your trials may taste bitter, but the Lord tastes better. O taste and see that the Lord is good (Psalm 34:8).*

Myrrh was a custom of the Jews to give those who were condemned to death by crucifixion. Wine mingled with myrrh was used to produce insensibility and was known to be numb pain.

The Lord is pouring oil and wine into all your wounds. God is drawing you out of your agony and granting you a fresh anointing. He's numbing your pain and bringing you to the place where you will hurt no more over things that have transpired in your past. The anointing of the Lord on you is greater than all the terrible things that have happened to you. As the oil flows through you, God's doing a quick work in you. Because of your pain, you are so much more powerful. You now have the power to tread upon serpents and scorpions. You have power over all the power of the enemy and nothing shall by any means harm you. Absolutely nothing! No man, no woman, no weapon, no words, no wind, no storm, no fire, no flood; absolutely nothing. It can't hurt you anymore and they can't harm you anymore. Nothing shall by any means harm you. The anointing is covering you. No weapon formed against you shall ever prosper and every tongue that rises against you in judgment shall be condemned (Isaiah 54:17). The weapon may form, but it will not prosper. You are anointed for THIS.

# CHAPTER 5

*God Has Not Forgotten*

# GOD HAS NOT FORGOTTEN

Have you ever been in a place in your life when things were going so wonderful? No worries, no problems, no issues, no burdens. Then all of a sudden everything takes a turn for the worse. We see an example of this very thing as read in 2 Samuel Chapter 4 and Chapter 9. Things were going well for a Mephibosheth, who was King Saul's grandson. He dwelt at Gibeah and abided in the royal residence. He lived in the palace, wanted for nothing and had everything he needed. Peace was within his walls and prosperity infiltrated his palace. He was living the blessed life and the best life, Royal

Kingdom Living. Then all of a sudden his grandfather's dynasty was attacked by assassins. Their adversaries pursued with the intent to wipe out Saul's entire family. When an enemy wants to destroy you he isn't just out to get you, but he's after your entire family.

At the time Mephibosheth was only five years old and was cared for by his nurse. Upon the onset of the sudden attack, his caregiver panics, picks up the young child and runs for their life. As she makes haste to escape their enemies, she flees in fear and ends up dropping Mephibosheth. She stumbles and he falls to the ground. He is injured and the damage was so great that he becomes paralyzed and immobilized. This tragedy happens at the age of five. Five represents grace and favour. He was in his year of favour then suddenly fatality confines him behind the bars of failure. It is important that you are extremely selective about who you allow to carry you. If they are not people that are strong in the faith, their fear can be the cause of your failure. They will drop you.

The feeling of being dropped is disappointing.

**It is important that you are extremely selective about who you allow to carry you. If they are not people that are strong in the faith, their fear can be the cause of your failure. They will drop you.**

When you allow another to carry you, there is a sense of trust and confidence that you have in their ability. You are relying on them to care for you, cover you and transport you to your destination safely. It's heartbreaking to trust in a person that you thought cared for you, all to be left in a state where they allow you to fall to the ground. You are left wondering, *"Why did they drop me? Why did they let me fall? If they really cared about me then why did they let me go?"* Sometimes people drop you simply because they don't have the capacity to carry you. When they are in trouble themselves sometimes there's simply no way they can carry both you and them. The burden becomes too great and the weight becomes too heavy. As they lose strength during times of distress they will drop you and you may end up injured or even crippled.

Mephibosheth became crippled as a result of the calamity. The bible says in 2 Samuel 4:4 that he is lame at the feet. He lost his ability to stand and the power to walk. This accident deprived him for life of the use of both feet. This one moment of noxiousness caused him to be deduced to living in permanent crippleness. To be crippled is to be disabled to the point where you are no longer able. This state can drive one into extreme misery. It's tormenting to have feet but unable to walk and to have legs but unable to stand. I can understand if you didn't have them, but to have something and cannot use it is frustrating and depressing.

Life started to rapidly decline for Mephibosheth. Injured and lame, he was carried to Lodebar and reared in the house of Machir. Lodebar is known to mean a place of no pasture, no bread and no word. Its meaning is interpreted as the Land of Nothing. He goes from a life of blessedness to breadlessness and nothingness. He is demoted from a palace where he has EVERYTHING and down to a pit where he has NOTHING. What a horrible transition to go from having everything down to nothing - no money, no food, without provision, no peace, no prosperity, no ability and most importantly no word.

It's one thing to be without things, but what's most miserable is to be in a place in life where you are without a Word from God. You can survive without bread, but you cannot live without the Word. The bible declares in Matthew 4:4 that, *"Man shall not live by bread alone, but by every Word that proceedeth out of the mouth of God."*

Lodebar is a place where you have nothing, not even a Word. You begin to feel lowly in your spirit and the devil tells you because you don't have nothing, you are nothing and you're never going to be nothing. Then he lies and tells you that God is not going to do nothing. The devil is a liar. God will not leave you in Lodebar. You probably feel empty, hurt, broken, worthless and wordless, but God has not forgotten. You searched for a Word when there was no Word to be found. You were in desperate need for a Word from the Lord, but you could find none. You prayed and no Word. You cried and no Word. You searched for a prophet and no Word. Your faith starts to decrease while hopelessness begins to increase. You needed God to speak, but you couldn't hear His voice. No Word nowhere to be found. You're trying to hold on the best you can and your soul begins to cry out, "All I need is a Word from the Lord." Your spirit knows that one Word can change everything. That's how powerful the Word of God is. It changes not just some things but everything. The whole universe and the entire earth is subject to the Word of the Lord. In Genesis 1:3 when God spoke a Word and said let there be light, there was light. Darkness itself had to bow and come subject to the authority of the Word. By Genesis 1:4, light was divided from darkness and darkness could no longer exist with the light. When light shines into darkness, darkness cannot overtake it. Darkness has no choice but to come subject, surrender and submit to the power of the Word. Your situation is subject to the Word, the Word is not subject to your situation. Until you get a Word, you will never be able to experience change in your situation. It's the Word of the Lord that changes everything.

Everything in your life is about to change. Your current condition is not your ultimate conclusion. Lodebar is not your final destination. It's just a temporary setback that God is using as a set up to bring you back up. You won't be down forever and it won't be like this always. Everything about your life is going to change for the better because you survived the worse. God has not forgotten about you. Others may forget, but God

---

## P❖WERP❖INT

**Your current condition is not your ultimate conclusion.**

won't. Sometimes because you're not in the place that you "had been", to others you become a "has been." People will forget you. They will be with you when you're up, but will disappear when you're down. After you have lost everything, they have no more need for you. This should provoke you to think, *"Were they with me because they wanted me or were they in my life for what they wanted from me."* Sometimes people really don't want you they just want what you have. In many instances people only do for you if you have the ability to do for them. The essence of real loyalty is when a person is committed to you during your times of abundant treasures and during moments of tragedy. Loyal people are not with you for what you have, they are glued to you because of who you are.

David was loyal to Saul and had a covenant relationship with Jonathan. David was a blessed man and received an unction to help somebody else. He asked, *"Is there yet any that is left of the house of Saul, that I may shew him kindness for Jonathan's sake?."* David is determined to bless Saul's offspring for Jonathan's sake. The word

left here in the text is interpreted as a remnant. Remnants are the left overs, the remains, the scraps and the fragmented pieces that persist after surviving devastation. The remnants are the proof that you've been through brokenness, but you're still here. You've been through disappointment, but you're still here. The devil tried to kill you, but you're still here. You didn't know how and if you were going to make it, but you're still here. Now God is going to take you to a place called "there." When you get to your "there" place, you are set free from having nothing and God will command the blessing. Psalm 133:3 says for "there" the Lord commanded the blessing. In your "there" place your blessing has no choice but to show up. What God has purposed to do for you isn't even about you. God's going to do it for Covenant's Sake. David had a covenant relationship with Jonathan; therefore he was committed to blessing his seed. The blessing was released for Covenant's Sake.

When life has been bad to you, God will raise up people that will take the time to be kind to you. Right now, at this very moment, someone is looking for you to bless you. God knows how to send the right person at the right time. They have exactly what you need to come out of where you've been. They are more concerned about where you're going and not stuck on where you're at. Their concern is getting you back to the place that you're supposed to be. David sends Saul's servant Ziba to go fetch Mephibosheth, Jonathan's son. Ziba knows his condition. He tells David that he's lame at his feet. Ziba knows where he's at (Lodedar meaning the Place of Nothingness) and who he's with (Machir meaning sold or given over to death). Ziba knew that Mephibosheth was lame, down to nothing, sitting in discouragement and given over into the hands of death. He knew the 411 and told the King all about it. King David sends the servant Ziba to go fetch him out of Lodebar. Fetch means to snatch completely out. God had already made a way of escape and pre-destined Mephibosheth's deliverance. God had not forgotten. The King sends Ziba to rescue stricken Mephibosheth out of bondage for the purpose of carrying him into his blessing. Ziba was a servant who symbolically represents one's Appointed Time. Time is a servant who works for the King. The King sent the lame remnant his appointed time to bring him completely out to never return again. I don't care how low you are or how long you've been where you are, when it's your appointed time you have to come out. Not only will you come out, but your ap-pointed time will snatch you out. The word snatch implies to take something up by force. Lodebar can-not hold you down because your appointed time is taking you up. It's your appointed time and your ap-pointed time is your set time. Favour is always re-leased during your set time. You've been frustrated and felt like a failure, but all of that is over. It's your set time to be favoured.

Mephibosheth is brought before the King and

the King speaks these words to him in 2 Samuel 9:7, *"And David said unto him, Fear not: for I will surely shew thee kindness for Jonathan thy father's sake, and will restore thee all the land of Saul thy father; and thou shalt eat bread at my table continually."* He promises to restore the blessings that were lost. He also promised him that he would eat at the King's Table continually, forever. Never again would he be without. He was coming out on broken pieces and total restoration was his portion. Mephibosheth felt so unworthy of the blessing because he felt so worthless. Mephibosheth asked the king why would he look on or consider blessing a dead dog such as himself. His mentality had not yet caught up with his reality. The reality was that he was no longer in Lodebar, but in the presence of the King. God is about to snatch you out so quickly that your mentality is going to have to rapidly catch up with your reality. Your mind can't remain stuck in nothing when your new reality is that the Lord has restored everything. Your mentality has to shift. Your mentality cannot be in Lodebar when your reality has been restored to luxury. When God elevates you to another level, you have to begin to think on another level. Your thinking has to change. You must shift your mind out of the discouragement and mentally let go of all the disappointment. Yes, you were disappointed because your life was scarce and you had nothing to eat, but now God's ushering you to a place where you can eat all you want. Thank God that He didn't forget about you.

# CHAPTER 6

# *I Made It Out On Broken Pieces*

# I Made It Out On Broken Pieces

As I look back over my life, there are so many difficult circumstances that I have faced. Often I wondered, "Lord how in the world did I make it out." The blows and the attacks that I've been hit with over the years many days seemed so unreal. The pain that I've experienced appeared to be so unendurable. I have experienced brokenness in my marriage, my family, my finances, my career and in ministry. I am very familiar with pain. I've been pierced in my heart and stabbed in my back. I've been betrayed by friends and assaulted by enemies. There was a time in my life where the adversary of my soul attacked my family so violently that it left me in a state of despair and tried to rob me of my willpower to live. The brokenness seemed so unbearable. The disaster looked extremely unfixable. I continued to ask the question, *"Lord how in the world am I going to make it out of this."* The answer is this: I made it out on broken pieces.

As we enter back into Acts Chapter 27, we see the outcome of the Apostle Paul's struggle. He experienced horrendous shipwreck. It looked like he wasn't going to survive. His calamity was outrageous and the violence of the storm was very atrocious. Though his survival didn't look promising, he still made it out. His safe escape was at stake because the ship began to break. Others on the ship wanted to vacate, but Paul warned them in Acts 27:31 that except they abide in the ship they would not be saved. They took heed to Paul's words and stayed on the ship. Then low and behold the ship still broke. Have you ever stayed in something that God said don't leave from and after you made the decision to stay that thing still broke? Maybe your cry is that you stayed in your marriage and it still broke. You stayed in a relationship and it still broke. You stayed in the house and it still broke. You stayed on your job and it still broke. You remained faithful, but everything around you shattered into pieces. What do you do when you stay and it still breaks? You would think that God would say leave if it's breaking and falling apart, but instead God says stay. It's hard to stay in anything when you know it's going to crumble. It would make since just to vanish and walk away. Anytime God tells you to stay in it, then you best believe He has a divine plan for it. He purposes to use what broke to bring you out.

Some situations you will never make it out of until it breaks. Paul stayed on the ship and the hinder part was broken by the violence of the waves. The ship began to break. They probably thought, *"What are we going to do now.?"* They were in a state of emergency and needed divine wisdom and supernatural courage to bring them through. When life is falling apart, you cannot make it by yourself. You need the wisdom of God and a Sovereign move of God to start working when it seems like nothing is going to work. God chooses the very thing that He purposes to use to rescue you and deliver you. Most of the time, God doesn't use the things we think; instead, He uses the things that we least expect. When Paul's ship broke and escaping looked impossible, God decided and predetermined to use the broken pieces to bring them all through.

According to Acts 27:43-44, the scriptures make clear both Paul's and the other prisoner's way of escape. The text reads, *"But the centurion, willing to save Paul, kept them from their purpose; and commanded that they which could swim should cast themselves first into the sea, and get to land: And the rest, some on boards, and some on broken pieces of the ship. And so it came to pass, that they escaped all safe to land."* Those that could swim were instructed to swim out. Some came out on boards and then there were others that made it out on broken pieces. Whenever God allows you to go through anything, before you go through it He already has designed your way of escape. Everybody doesn't come out the same. One person may swim their way out, but you may have to use the thing that broke to make it out.

God is so amazing that He can use your breakdown as a vehicle to carry you into your breakthrough. Thank Him for what fell apart and for the things that were tore up in your life. Though you thought you were going to die in it, God was using

**God is so amazing that He can use your breakdown as a vehicle to carry you into your breakthrough.**

the brokenness to get you out of it. If the ship would not have broken, many would have sunk. The Lord wants to use your brokenness to help you escape. Thank God that it broke. It's easy to praise God for what He kept together, but praise Him for the things that fell apart. If it had not collapsed and fallen to pieces, you would still be bound in it. It had to break so that you could get out.

There is a blessing in brokenness. Jesus breaks five loaves of bread and two fish in order to bring a multitude out of hunger. Four men endeavored to get a lame man who was stricken with palsy to Jesus to be healed. They tried to go through the door to get the man to the Master, but there was no room so the men went another way. They bore the crippled man up the roof and the break the roof up in order to lower the man down into the presence of God (Jesus). There is a blessing in brokenness. Elisha breaks a stick and throws it in the water in order to rescue a lost axe head that was dropped. When the broken stick hit the Jordan River, the axe head was recovered. It did supernaturally swim its way back. Multiplication and miracles are released in the breaking.

Sometimes the only way to get something out is to break it out. In Matthew 14:3, there was a woman with the alabaster box filled with spikenard that anointed Jesus. She had been storing up this costly, expensive oil in her treasure box for years. She desired to pour her love the Lord so she broke the box in order to get the oil out. When God is anointing you for a breakthrough and trying to get oil out of you, there has to be a breaking that takes place within you. Breakthrough cannot happen without a breaking. Something has to break in order for you to get through. This is the blessing of brokenness.

P❖WERP❖INT

**Breakthrough cannot happen without a breaking. Something has to break in order for you to get through.**

The conclusion of Paul's story and the testimony of victory is found in Acts 27:44. This bible says, *"...And so it came to pass, that they escaped all safe to land."* The shipwreck was disastrous, but what God had purposed still came to pass. Despite the storms of life, what God said will come to pass. It was impossible for peril to stop God's purpose. Even though you've been opposed by destruction, God's plan for you cannot be destroyed. The Lord had predestined for them to survive. All those that were on the ship escaped. They were preserved from danger and made it safely to land. This is the epitome of salvation and deliverance. The Lord made a way out of no way. He's made a way for you and your brokenness is going to bring you through. You're going to make it out on broken pieces.

Right after the Apostle Paul survives shipwreck and makes it out on broken pieces, he makes it to dry land safely. He arrives to an island called Malta. Keep in mind, his initial objective for the voyage was to be freed from the Justice System and released from prison. When they arrived to Malta, it was cold and rainy and the people lit a fire to keep warm. As Paul laid sticks on the fire, a poisonous snake, driven out by the heat, fastened itself onto his hand. The people of the island waited for Paul to swell up and die. Paul shook the snake in the fire and was completely without harm. Whatever has gripped your life, use the fire to your advantage and shake it off. When Paul shook the beast into the fire, he shook off more than a snake – he shook off an entire demonic system. According to Acts 28:4 (NIV), the snake has a name.

*"When the islanders saw the snake hanging from his hand, they said to each other, "This man must be a murderer; for though he escaped from the sea, Justice has not allowed him to live." – Acts 28:4 NIV*

The snake's name is Justice. Justice was the demonic system that treated Paul unfairly and imprisoned him wrongly – he was simply doing the work of the Lord Jesus Christ. When Paul shook the snake into the fire, he literally shook the Justice System off of his life that was practicing injustice against him. This demonic system was cast into the fire.

Whatever demonic, oppressive system that has

gripped your life, you have the power to shake it off. Let the fire of God burn in your life and allow this fire to burn away everything that tried to poison you, kill you and utterly destroy you. Maybe you were mistreated and done very wrongly. You don't have time to carry the pain of it; shake it off. You've come too far to allow the snake bite to poison you. If the storm couldn't destroy you, then surely the snake cannot kill you. You may have been bitten, but thank God you weren't poisoned. You are free from the power of injustice and the Lord is going to vindicate you for how others have mishandled you. For every snake that rose up against you, the Lord shall repay them and He will recompense you. The Lord Himself shall be your exceeding great reward.

# CHAPTER 7

*From A Broken Piece
To A Masterpiece*

# FROM A BROKEN PIECE TO A MASTERPIECE

I f you've been broken by the winds of life, then you qualify for God to put you back together. There is never a need to put anything together that's already perfectly together. The saying goes, if it's not broken then don't fix it. He's fixing you because you've been broken. God is the potter and we are the clay. He desires to remake us, remold us, renew us and restore us. We are his handiwork and He's reaching His hand into our lives and taking all of our broken pieces and turning them into masterpieces. It's not the will of the Father for His people to remain fragmented and in broken pieces. He desires to restore you back to His masterpiece. According to Ephesians 2:10 NLT that's what you were destined to be, A Masterpiece. *"For we are God's masterpiece. He has created us anew in Christ Jesus, so we can do the good things he planned for us long ago."*

A masterpiece is a craftsman's greatest piece of work. We are God's greatest piece of work. The Angels are even mesmerized by us. They are in awe over our existence and marvel about how God feels about us. We are God's outstanding work of achievement and they asked the Lord, *"What is it about man that you're so mindful of?"* You and I are an expression of the Master's creativity. Only a Master Craftsman can take the dust of the earth and make man in His image and after His very likeness. Out of the dirt and from the lowest part of the earth, He formed our identity and made us to look just like Him. The Creator Himself reached down, just to build us up that we might become the Masterpiece He purposed for us to be.

A diamond is a wonderful example of a Masterpiece. Diamonds begin as broken pieces but are transformed into Masterpieces. Diamonds are made deep within the darkness of the earth under high crushing pressure and extreme temperatures that enable them to form. They are made out of the rough. If you're ever going to be a diamond, you must be able to endure times of deep darkness and press through your process even when things are rough. Darkness is needful when it comes to one's development. A snapshot of a beautiful picture is developed into a stunning portrait in the Dark Room. It's through the dark times of life that God uses to develop us into the full essence of what He has purposed for us to become. If you are afraid of darkness, then don't expect to be developed. It's out of obscurity are we matured into mighty overcomers. Until we can applaud our process while in darkness, we will never appreciate when He breaks us forth into His marvelous light. Moreover, not only do diamonds emerge out of darkness into the light, they also disperse light. This gemstone acts like a prism and has the ability to separate white light into rainbow colors. A rainbow is indicative of the promises of God. A real diamond has a way of shining through the light of pain and turning the color of pain into a manifested promise. To a diamond, pain is a prophetic signal that I am real close to what God promised.

The Rough is a place that the Master takes our broken pieces through process and transforms them into amazing Masterpieces. Everything great must go through process. Process is interchangeable with progress. There can never be any true progress without undergoing the necessary process. Like a diamond, the process is very extreme. No diamond is made without pressure and heat. If you can't take the pressure or endure the heat, then you're not Diamond Material. To create a diamond it requires approximately 650,000-750,000 pounds of pressure per square inch. The temperature has to be at least 1700 – 2400 degrees Fahrenheit. This is some intense pressure and some serious heat. Both the pressure and the heat are necessary in order for the diamond to emerge. The reason why you have experienced so much pressure is because God is making you. You're a diamond out of the rough and destined to be placed as a dazzling array on public display. God desires to make you showcase ready. You're going to be stellar and stunning; lustrous and lovely, from a broken piece to a masterpiece. You're about to be a head-turner, an eye-catcher, attention-getter and an atmosphere-shifter. When others gaze into the window of your life, you are going to take their breath away because the incandescence of your shine. Your value is increasing and the pain of your past is decreasing. You are far work more than others have given you credit for. Those that have hurt you in the past knew your value but never wanted you to realize it. They attempted to damage you to diminish your self-worth so that you could never become aware of how much you're truly worth. No longer will yesterday's brokenness hinder you from being a testimony of God's brilliancy. It's your time to arise and shine for the light has come and the glory of the Lord is risen upon you.

You've been through so many things and the question yet remains, *"How did I really make it out?"* It's because you were intrinsically designed with an unusual strength. A diamond actually symbolizes strength, being the hardest substance in the world, and is thus the perfect representation endurance. The word "diamond" itself is derived from the Greek word "adamas," which means indestructible and unconquerable. It's just not in you to be destroyed or conquered and that's why you're still alive. The tears you've cried couldn't drown you, the devastation couldn't kill you, the attack couldn't destroy you, and the heartache couldn't conquer you. You were built to last and born to win. I know it's been rough, but when the Master gets done with you, you'll be amazed by His accomplished work of art. Jehovah Elohim, God our Creator, is going to give you beauty for ashes and out of the ashes your beauty will rise. The Master is eager to put His Masterpiece on display because the world is longing to see a manifestation of the restored, better you.

God is making you bigger and everything about you is getting better. When you were broken the assassin of your soul meant it for evil, but God meant it unto good. This is Joseph's testimony in Genesis 50:20. After being thrown in a pit, sold into slavery, locked up in prison, Joseph still had a "But God" in His spirit. "But" is that which is contrary to what another expected. The devil expected one thing, but God had already purposed another. Joseph's brothers, who threw him in the pit, never imagined that the favour of God would elevate him to the palace. God's purposes are sure, His plans are preeminent and all His promises are yea and Amen. But God!

---

"But" is also the lead into the positive after the negative. Keep declaring "But God" and every time you proclaim it you are literally shifting all life's negatives and transforming them into positives. When you declare "But God" you're shifting your pain into promises, your weaknesses into strength, your sorrows into joy and your morning into dancing. Stop praising your pain and quit worshipping your wounds. Refuse to give the adversary credit for the disasters that have happened against you and praise Jesus for the incredible things that are happening for you. The trajectory of your life is ordained by the Lord. To God be all the glory for the things that He has done. Not once did he allow the shipwreck to destroy you. He allowed your ship to break to give you a way out of the storm. 1 Corinthians 10:13 sums up all your struggles and the purpose of your many tests. This verse in the

Amplified Bible reads,

> "For no temptation (no trial regarded as enticing
> to sin), [no matter how it comes or where it leads]
> has overtaken you and laid hold on you that is not
> common to man [that is, no temptation or trial
> has come to you that is beyond human resistance
> and that is not adjusted and adapted and belong-
> ing to human experience, and such as man can
> bear]. But God is faithful [to His Word and to His
> compassionate nature], and He [can be trusted]
> not to let you be tempted and tried and assayed
> beyond your ability and strength of resistance and
> power to endure, but with the temptation He will
> [always] also provide the way out (the means of
> escape to a landing place), that you may be capa-
> ble and strong and powerful to bear up under it
> patiently."

There are so many power points in this verse.
The first point is that no trial has ever or will ever
come to you that is beyond your level of human re-
sistance. You have the power in you to resist the devil
and he will have to flee. Secondly, God will never al-

P✻WERP✻INT

**God will not allow your problem to be bigger than your power. Your power will always be much larger than your problem.**

low you to be tested above your ability to endure. God will not allow your problem to be bigger than your power. Your power will always be much larger than your problem. Thirdly, with the temptation, the test and the trial, God provides the means of escape to a landing place. The way out comes along "with" the temptation. They are a package deal, they work together. So what you're in (the test, the trial, the problem) persists simultaneously with your way out (the escape plan).

In conclusion, God will never allow you to go through anything without already making your way of escape in advance. Before you got in it, God already had a plan to get you out of it. You made it out on broken pieces and the Master is taking all your broken pieces and turning them into Masterpieces. After He completes you, you won't look like what you've been through. Stay ready for the greater. What's to come is better than what's been.

Made in the USA
Charleston, SC
21 December 2016